Contents

As we live in a rapidly changing society, exposure to and fluency in Science, Technology, Engineering, and Mathematics (STEM) ensures students will gain the skills they will need to succeed in the 21st century. It is essential that students gain practice in becoming good problem solvers, critical thinkers, innovators, inventors, and risk takers.

Teacher Tips

Encourage Topic Interest

Help students develop an understanding and appreciation of different STEM concepts by providing an area in the classroom to display topic-related non-fiction books, pictures, collections, and artifacts as a springboard for learning.

What I Think I Know / What I Would Like to Know Activity

Introduce each STEM unit by asking students what they think they know about the topic, and what they would like to know about the topic. Complete this activity as a whole-group brainstorming session, in cooperative small groups, or independently. Once students have had a chance to complete the questions, combine the information to create a class chart for display. Throughout the study, periodically update students' progress in accomplishing their goal of what they want to know, and validate what they think they know.

Vocabulary List

Keep track of new and content-related vocabulary on chart paper for students' reference. Encourage students to add words to the list. Classify the word list into the categories of nouns, verbs, and adjectives. In addition, have students create their own science dictionaries as part of their learning logs.

Learning Logs

Keeping a learning log is an effective way for students to organize thoughts and ideas about the STEM concepts presented and examined. Students' learning logs also provide insight on what follow-up activities are needed to review and to clarify concepts learned.

Learning logs can include the following types of entries:

- Teacher prompts
- Students' personal reflections
- Questions that arise
- Connections discovered
- Labeled diagrams and pictures
- Definitions for new vocabulary

Mammals Are Animals

There are different types of animals.
Some animals are **mammals**.

Mammal Facts

- Mammals are warm blooded.
- Mammals have hair or fur.
- Mammal babies are born alive.
- Mammals produce milk to feed their babies.

Most mammals live on land.

Polar bears live in
very cold places.

Camels live in
very hot places.

Moles live under
the ground.

Did you know that bats are the only
mammals that can fly?

Mammals such as whales
live in water.

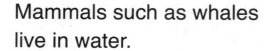

2

"Mammals Are Animals"—Think About It!

1. How can you tell a raccoon is a mammal?
List four ways.

• He has fur.

• Racoons are warm blooded

• Racoons give birth

• Rcoons are mammals

2. Name three mammals.

cats

dogs

hamsters

3. Choose a mammal that you like. Tell three things about it. Read the
clues to your friends. Did they guess the mammal?

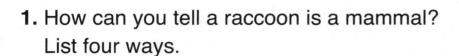

Cat

It gives burth.

It feeds milk to its babies.

And is super cute.

Other Kinds of Animals

Read the chart to learn about other kinds of animals.

Kind of Animal	Features
Birds owl	• Birds have two legs. • They have a beak but no teeth. • Most birds can fly using wings. • Birds hatch from eggs.
Insects grasshopper	• Insects have six legs. • Most insects can fly using wings. • Insects hatch from eggs.
Fish salmon	• Fish live in water. • They have fins to help them swim. • They have gills to breathe. • Fish hatch from eggs.
Amphibians frog	• Amphibians usually live first in water, then later on land. • They hatch from eggs.
Reptiles turtle	• Turtles live in water and on land. • Lizards live on land. • Most reptiles hatch from eggs.

Classify Animals Game

1. Create a word card for each type of animal:

amphibians   **birds**   **fish**   **insects**   **mammals**   **reptiles**

2. Color and cut out the picture cards.

3. Spread out the word cards you created. Sort the picture cards by type of animal.

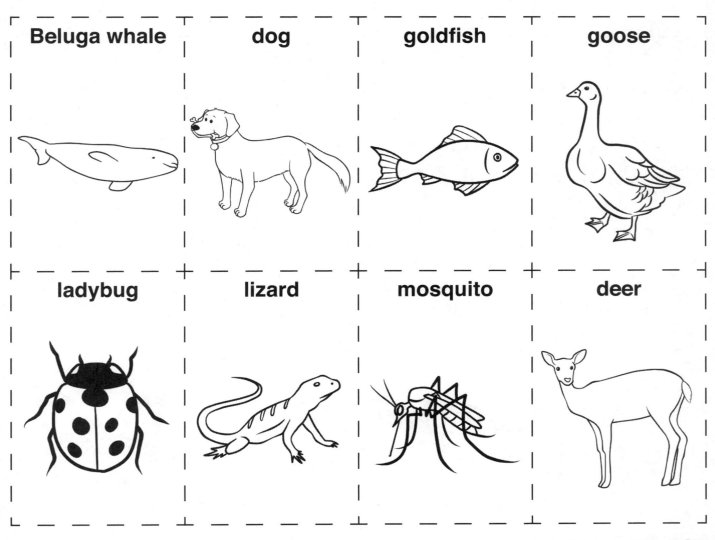

| **Beluga whale** | **dog** | **goldfish** | **goose** |
| **ladybug** | **lizard** | **mosquito** | **deer** |

continued next page ☞

frog	shark	bee	duck
snake	beetle	squirrel	crocodile
bluebird	turtle	ant	butterfly

Animals Grow Up

Animals go through stages to grow up. The stages make a life cycle. Most animals have a simple life cycle. They are born alive from their mother or hatch from eggs. Then they grow to adult size.

The life cycle of an elephant and a mouse are similar. Both are born alive from their mother. They drink milk from their mother. They look like their parents, but are smaller. Both will grow up and look even more like their parents. The human life cycle is similar to that of elephants and mice.

Amphibians have more stages in their life cycle. They go through big changes. Look at the pictures that show how frogs grow and change.

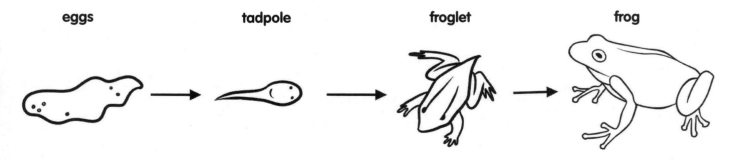

eggs   **tadpole**   **froglet**   **frog**

A tadpole hatches from an egg. The tadpole has gills like a fish to breathe in the water. It grows slowly into a froglet, then into a frog. The frog lives on land and breathes air the same way you do.

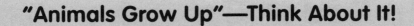

"Animals Grow Up"—Think About It!

1. The diagram shows the life cycle of the frog. Use the words below to label the diagram.

eggs   frog   froglet   tadpole

_____

A tadpole hatches out of each egg. The tadpole has a long tail but no legs. Is has gills to breathe in the water.

A mother frog lays her eggs in water.

_____

As a tadpole grows, its hind legs begin to grow. Its tail becomes shorter and disappears. The froglet begins to breathe air.

_____

The frog leaves the water. It can now live on land. After three years, the cycle starts again.

2. How many stages are there in the life cycle of a frog?

_____

continued next page ☞

Some baby animals look just like their parents. Some animals change just a little as they grow up. Other animals change a lot as they grow.

Draw a line to match the baby to the adult.

3.

4.

5.

6

7.

A.

B.

C.

D.

E.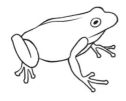

Brain Stretch

On a sheet of paper, draw the life cycle of a chicken. There are three stages. The stages are egg, chick, and chicken. Label your sketch. Write what you know about each stage.

Animals Are Built to Live

Animals have to do many things to live. They have to find food and water. Animals have to be able to move. They have to build homes. They also must keep safe.

Animals have special features to help them survive. These features are called adaptations.

Body Adaptations

Some animals have special body parts. The chart shows some body adaptations.

Frogs use their long, sticky tongues to catch flies. 	Ducks have webbed feet that help them swim. 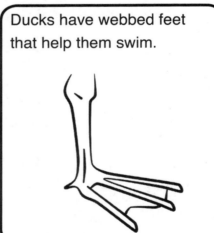	Insects use their wings to fly. 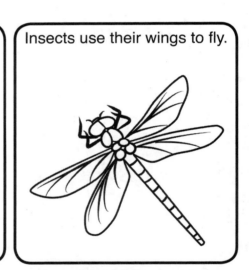
Crabs have sharp claws to catch food. 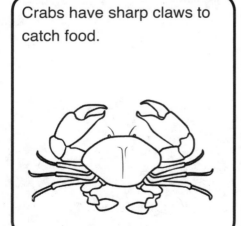	Whales use flippers to help turn and steer in the water. 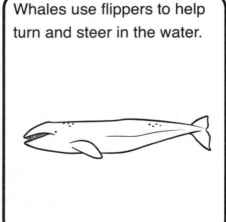	Cats use their whiskers to feel what is nearby. This helps cats find their way in the dark. 

"Animals Are Built to Live"—Think About It!

1. Fill in the blank.

A whale's body is built for the cold. It has blubber to keep warm.
Blubber is a layer of fat under the skin. Blubber is an

_____ .

2. What is an adaptation? Give one example.

_____

_____

_____

3. Invent an animal with two adaptations. Draw the animal. Label
the adaptations.

Body Coverings

Body coverings are adaptations. Body coverings such as skin protect animals. Skin helps animals stay warm and dry.

Hair and Fur

Most mammals have skin covered with hair or fur. Your skin is covered with hair!

Fur A polar bear has skin covered with thick fur. This helps the bear stay warm.

Hair An elephant has only a little bit of hair. This helps pull heat away from its body.

Wet Skin Amphibians such as frogs have thin, wet skin. This helps them breathe.

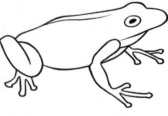

Feathers Birds have skin covered with feathers. Feathers help birds stay warm and dry. They also help birds fly.

Scales Fish have skin covered with wet scales. The scales protect the skin.

Shells Insects have a shell but no skin. The shell is dry and hard. The shell helps keep the beetle from drying out.

"Body Coverings"—Think About It!

1. List two types of body coverings that help animals.

_____   _____

2. Turtles are the only reptiles that have shells. How do you think a shell helps a turtle?

_____

_____

_____

Read each sentence. Write the name of one animal that matches the description.

3. I have fur. _____

4. I have dry scales. _____

5. I have feathers. _____

6. I have wet scales. _____

7. I have wet skin. _____

8. I have a shell. _____

9. Did you know that porcupines have quills growing from their skin? What might the quills be used for?

_____

_____

Animals Hide

Some animals blend in with their surroundings. This adaptation is called camouflage. Animals use camouflage to hide from other animals. Here are some ways that animals use camouflage.

Color: Some animals are the same color as their surroundings. A snowy owl is white and lives where it snows. It blends in with the snow.

Pattern: Some animals have stripes, spots, or other patterns on their skin. The spots on a leopard help it hide in tall grasses. The stripes on a zebra make it difficult to see one zebra in a herd.

Mimicry: Some animals look like something else. A walking stick is an insect that looks like a twig. The leaf katydid is an insect that looks like a leaf.

Some animals use color and patterns to look like an animal that is dangerous. This is called **mimicry**.

The Viceroy butterfly looks like a Monarch butterfly. The Monarch butterfly is poisonous. Animals leave both butterflies alone!

"Animals Hide"—Think About It!

1. Why do animals use camouflage?

_____

_____

_____

2. What do these animals use to blend in with their surroundings?
Complete the Venn diagram. Use the words below.

bumblebee   **giraffe**   **Arctic hare**   **Polar bear**   **Artic fox**
Snowy owl   **tiger**   **White-tailed deer**   **zebra**

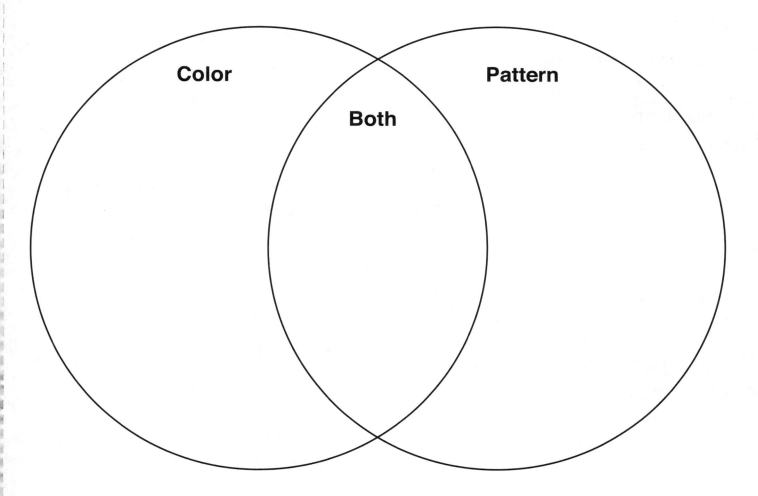

Animals Adapt to the Seasons

Some animals adapt to changes in the seasons.

Color Changes

Some animals change the color of their coats to match the season. In the summer, the Arctic fox sheds its white coat for a brown coat.

The Arctic hare has a brown coat in the spring and summer. Its coat blends in with the surroundings. In the fall and winter, the hare has a white coat to blend in with the snow.

Migration

Many birds such as hummingbirds fly to warmer places for the winter. This is called migration.

Some animals such as deer migrate in large herds to warmer places.

Hibernation

Some animals hibernate, or sleep, during the winter. Animals hibernate in different ways. Bears sleep most of the winter without waking up.

In winter, a squirrel sleeps for a few days at a time. It wakes up to eat some food. Then it goes back to sleep.

"Animals Adapt to the Seasons"—Think About It!

Circle true or false for questions 1 to 3.

1. Some animals change color to match the season.   **True   False**

2. Many birds fly north for the winter.   **True   False**

3. Some animals hibernate during the winter.   **True   False**

4. Use red to circle the animals that migrate.
   Use blue to circle the animals that hibernate.
   Use green to circle the animals that change the color of their coat in winter.

butterfly 	**squirrel** 	**Arctic fox** 
bear 	**Arctic hare** 	**deer** 

Animals Help Us

Read about how animals help people.

People use animals for food.

We get eggs and meat from chickens.

People make useful things from animals.

We use wool from sheep to make clothes and blankets.

People depend on bees to help plants make food. Bees also make honey.

Bees visit flowers. This helps plants make seeds. Seeds grow into fruits that we eat such as pears.

Some people depend on animals such as donkeys to carry things.

Guide dogs help people who cannot see or cannot hear.

18

1. Complete the wheel.

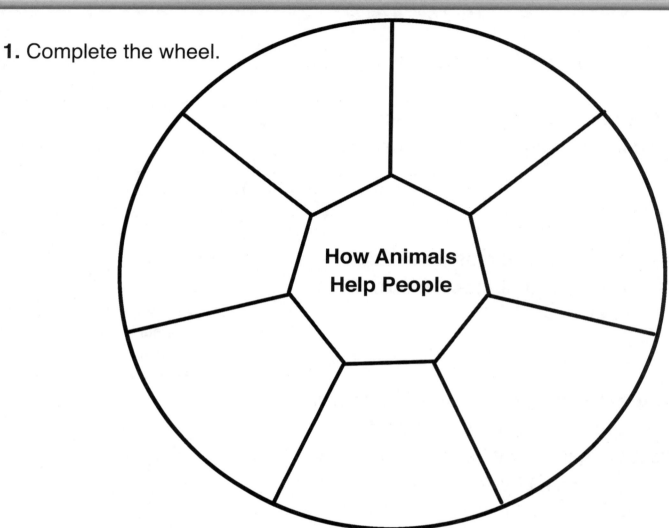

How Animals
Help People

2. Think of two things that people get from cows. Explain how these things are helpful.

_____

_____

3. Did you know that dragonflies eat mosquitoes? So do bats. How does this help people?

_____

_____

Animals Can Harm Us

Read about how animals can harm people.

Injuries: Some animals are dangerous. They can bite, scratch, or claw people.

Diseases: Ticks and mosquitoes can spread diseases that make people sick.

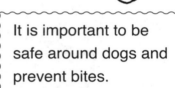

It is important to be safe around dogs and prevent bites.

Allergies: Some people sneeze and have trouble breathing when they are near certain animals. They have an allergy to the animal. Insect bites and bee stings can cause a rash or itching.

Pests: Some animals harm crops. Deer eat plants in gardens. Birds eat fruit such as berries. Insects such as beetles and grasshoppers eat grains. Termites and ants eat wood in our homes.

Some people are allergic to cats.

"Animals Can Harm Us"—Think About It!

Draw a line from the animal to its description.

1. grasshopper

A. I can spread diseases that make you sick.

2. bee

B. I can claw and bite people.

3. cat

C. I eat plants in your garden.

4. mosquito

D. I like to eat wheat.

5. deer

E. I make some people sneeze.

6. bear

F. I eat the wood in your woodpile.

7. termite

G. My sting can make you very itchy.

Helpful or Harmful?

Draw a happy face if the picture shows a way that people help animals.
Draw a sad face if the picture shows a way that people harm animals.

Helpful or Harmful?	Draw a Face
1. 	
2. 	
3.  Give Me a Home	

Animals in Danger!

Some animals are extinct. This means these animals no longer exist anywhere in the world. Some animals are endangered. This means they are in danger of becoming extinct.

Burrowing Owls

Burrowing owls are one of the smallest types of owls in the United States. They live in the ground in old badger and ground squirrel burrows. These owls eat mice, grasshoppers, and beetles. They are endangered because there are fewer animals to make the burrows. Farming and building houses and businesses also destroys the burrows.

Burrowing owl

Beluga Whales

Beluga whales live in the Arctic and the St. Lawrence River. They eat fish and other sea animals. They give birth to their young in the summer. They come into rivers to do this. They are endangered mostly because people hunted them for food. Today people limit hunting to protect the whales.

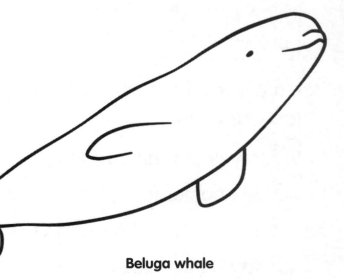

Beluga whale

"Animals in Danger!"—Think About It!

1. Choose one animal that is endangered.

_____

2. Use the chart to write about the animal.

What does the animal look like?	
Where does the animal live?	
What does the animal eat?	
What are the animal's special features?	
What is an interesting fact about the animal?	
Why is the animal endangered?	
How can people help protect the animal?	

3. On a sheet of paper, make a poster about the animal. Use the checklist for your poster.

☐ My poster has a title.

☐ My poster tells why the animal is endangered.

☐ My poster asks people to help save the animal.

☐ My printing is easy to read.

☐ My poster includes a picture.

Matter Is Everywhere

Look around you. How are juice, a horse, and steam alike? They are all made of matter. Matter is anything that takes up space and has mass. Everything can be sorted into one of three states of matter: solid, liquid, or gas.

Matter can be in the solid state.

Matter can be in the liquid state.

Matter can be in the gas state.

Think About It!

1. What are the three states of matter?

_____ , _____ , _____

2. Give an example of a solid. _____

3. Give an example of a liquid. _____

4. Give an example of a gas. _____

Solids

Did you know there are different types of solids?

Some solids are hard.
Ice and books are solids.

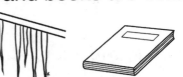

Some solids are soft.
Feathers and pillows are solids.

Rocks and leaves are solids found in nature.

Solid Facts

- Solids take up space. The amount of space does not change.
- Solids keep the same shape.
- Solids can break, but they are still solid.

Think About It!

1. Give an example of a solid that is hard. _____

2. Give an example of a solid that is soft. _____

3. Give an example of a solid found in nature. _____

4. Is a baseball a solid? How do you know?

_____

Solids Collage

Look in magazines for pictures of solids. Look for words describing solids, too. Cut out the pictures. Paste them below to make a collage.

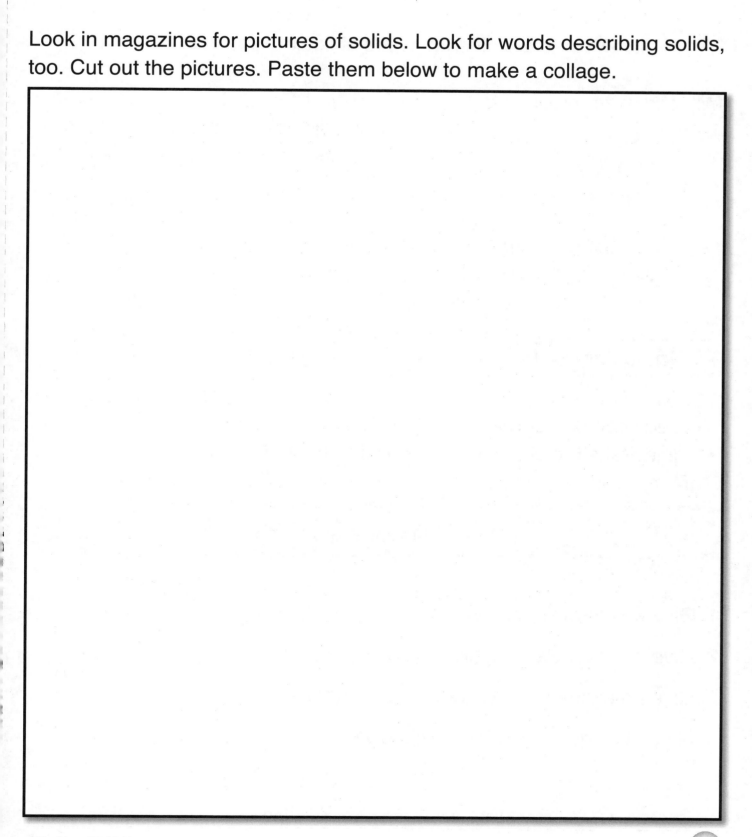

Liquids

Did you know there are different types of liquids?

Milk and water are liquids.

Some liquids are thick such as maple syrup.

Rain and tree sap are liquids found in nature.

Liquid Facts

- Liquids flow.
- Liquids can be poured.
- Liquids take the shape of the container they are in.

Think About It!

1. Give an example of a liquid. _____

2. Give an example of a thick liquid. _____

3. Give an example of a liquid found in nature. _____

4. Is paint a liquid? How do you know?

_____

_____

Liquids Collage

Look in magazines for pictures of liquids. Look for words describing liquids, too. Cut out the pictures. Paste them below to make a collage.

Experiment: Will It Change?

Test liquids and solids. See if they will change state.

Type of Liquid: _____

Test	Prediction: Will it change?	Observation: Did it change?
What happens when you put it in the freezer?		
What happens when you heat it?		
What happens when you pour it?		
What happens when you stir it?		

Type of Solid: _____

Test	Prediction: Will it change?	Observation: Did it change?
What happens when you put it in the freezer?		
What happens when you heat it?		
What happens when you pour it?		
What happens when you stir it?		

Compare and Contrast

When you compare something, look for what is the same. When you contrast something, look for what is different.

Find items to compare. They might be two liquids. They might be two solids. Or they might be a liquid and solid. Write what the items are:

_____ and _____

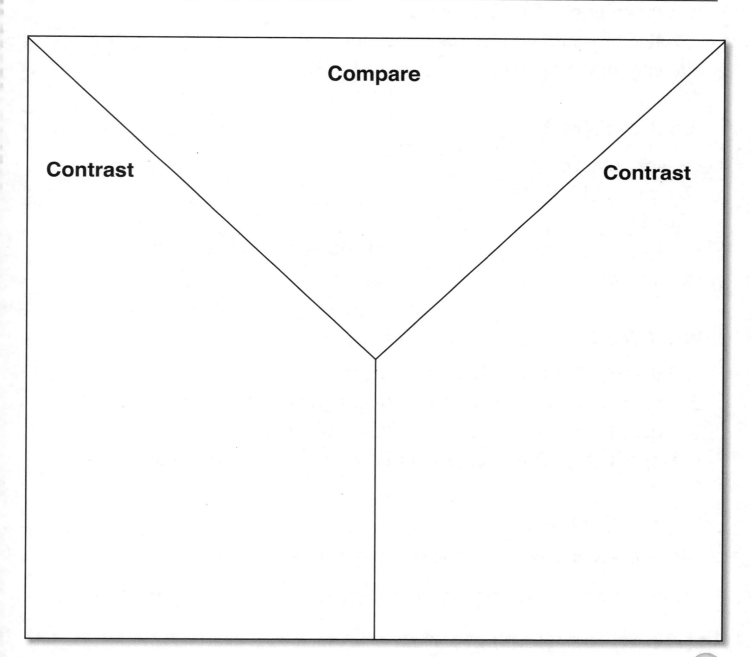

Experiment: Mix It Up

What happens when you mix milk and chocolate powder? Mmm, chocolate milk! The chocolate powder dissolves in the milk.

When you mix water and flour together, you make paste. Do other solids dissolve in water? Record your predictions then find out with this experiment.

What You Need

- 6 clear plastic cups
- 51 oz (1.5 L) of water
- Spoon
- 1 tsp (5 ml) each of sugar, salt, baking soda, pepper, sand
- 2 marbles

What You Do

1. Fill each plastic cup half full of water.
2. Using your spoon, stir one solid substance into one cup of water.
3. Record what you see. Use words or pictures.
4. Repeat steps 2 and 3, putting each solid into its own cup.

What Happened?

Circle the solids that dissolved when mixed with water.

sugar   **salt**   **baking soda**   **pepper**   **sand**   **marbles**

Experiment: Big Stuff

Does water take up more space when it is liquid or when it is ice?
Follow these steps to find out.

What You Need

- Small plastic bottle
- Water
- Aluminum foil
- Freezer

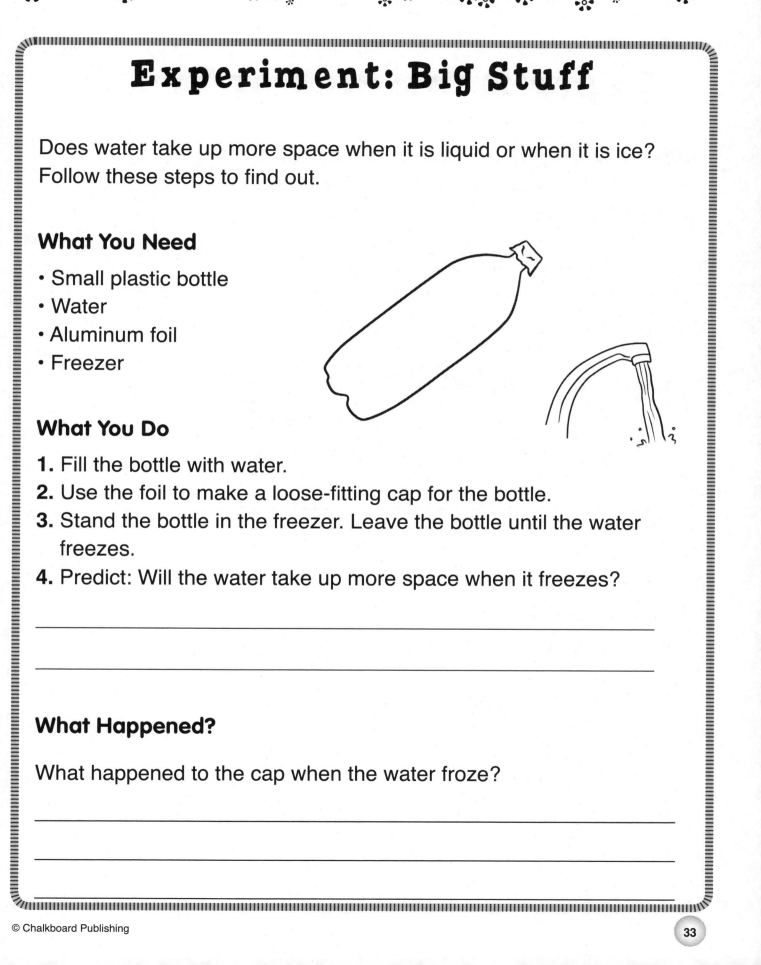

What You Do

1. Fill the bottle with water.
2. Use the foil to make a loose-fitting cap for the bottle.
3. Stand the bottle in the freezer. Leave the bottle until the water freezes.
4. Predict: Will the water take up more space when it freezes?

_____

_____

What Happened?

What happened to the cap when the water froze?

_____

_____

Experiment: Sink or Float?

When a solid floats, it is buoyant. Boats, rafts, and other things that float on water are buoyant. Not all solids float.

Test the solids below in a tub of water. Circle what you think will happen. Then, circle what you see happen.

Solid	Prediction	Observation
marble	sink float	sinks floats
feather	sink float	sinks floats
coin	sink float	sinks floats
button	sink float	sinks floats
paper	sink float	sinks floats

What Happened?

Were your predictions accurate? What surprised you?

_____

_____

_____

_____

_____

Experiment: Soak It Up!

What a mess! There is water everywhere!
How will you clean it up? Materials that soak
up liquid are absorbent. Not all solids can
absorb liquids. Some solids repel liquid.
Repel means push away.

Test the solids below. Will they absorb or
repel water? Circle what you think will happen.
Then, circle what you see happen.

Solid	Prediction	Observation
paper	absorb repel	absorbs repels
sponge	absorb repel	absorbs repels
plastic	absorb repel	absorbs repels
waxed paper	absorb repel	absorbs repels
cloth	absorb repel	absorbs repels

What Happened?

Rank the solids from most absorbent to least absorbent.

1. _____

2. _____

3. _____

4. _____

5. _____

Experiment: The Layered Look

If you pour water and grape juice into the same glass, they mix. Not all liquids will mix. Some liquids form layers.

Some solid objects will float on these layers of liquids. Other objects will sink. Try this activity to find out more about floating and sinking.

What You Need

- Tall clear jar
- 1/2 cup (125 ml) corn syrup
- 1/2 cup (125 ml) cooking oil
- 1/2 cup (125 ml) water
- Solid objects such as a cork, a small toy, a building block, a raisin, an ice cube

Tip: Dye the liquids with food coloring to more easily see the layers.

What You Do

1. Pour the corn syrup into the jar.
2. Carefully pour the oil into the jar.
3. Carefully pour the water into the jar.
4. Carefully add the objects to the jar.

What Happened?

On the jar diagram, record what you see.
Label the diagram.

Rain and Sleet

Rain is a liquid that falls from the sky. If the weather is cold enough, rain can freeze and become a solid. Rain can become freezing rain, sleet, or hail. Sleet is tiny pellets of ice that is sometimes mixed with rain or snow. Hail is balls of ice.

When freezing rain falls, sidewalks and roads become very icy. You have to walk very carefully so you do not slip and fall.

Icy Times

Freezing rain and sleet can affect people in many ways. Driving a car is very difficult when roads are covered with sleet. The roads are icy and slippery.

Freezing rain can also damage trees. Branches coated with ice can be very heavy. That can make them break off and fall.

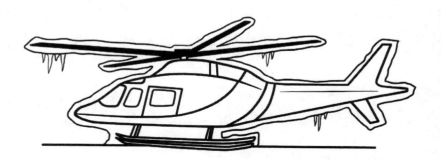

Layers of ice can also build up on electrical wires. They may also break and fall down. That means homes and other buildings would not have power.

Think About It!

Use another sheet of paper to write a story about freezing rain. It can be something you imagine, or something you remember.

Liquids and Solids Every Day

You pour a glass of water. You bite into a juicy apple. You drink and eat many liquids and solids every day.

You use liquids and solids in many other ways. If you have a bad cold, you might swallow liquid or solid medicine. It is important to take medicine carefully. Ask an adult to read the package. Never take someone else's medicine.

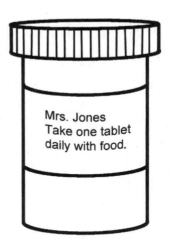

Mrs. Jones
Take one tablet
daily with food.

Cleanup Time

Water is a great help when cleaning up a mess. Sometimes you also need a bar of soap. A sponge is a solid that can help clean up. Liquids and solids can help you clean many things.

Some cleaning liquids and solids are poisonous. They should be stored carefully and put where young children cannot reach them.

Think About It!

Think about your day.

1. List four solids you used.

_____   _____

_____   _____

2. List three liquids you used.

_____   _____

_____

Stay Safe

Some liquids and solids are dangerous. Some can burn you. Others can harm lakes and rivers. Some liquids and solids can poison animals.

These are some symbols you may see on dangerous liquids and solids. Ask an adult for help if you see these symbols.

This symbol means what is inside can burn your skin. Bottles of bleach have this symbol.

This symbol means poison is inside. Detergents and other cleaners have this symbol.

This symbol means what is inside can catch fire. This symbol is on hairspray and oven cleaner.

1. Tell how safety symbols help keep people safe. Use information from the reading and your own ideas.

_____

_____

_____

_____

2. Never put a dangerous substance in a different container. Explain why this is dangerous.

_____

_____

3. Match each safety symbol to its meaning.

Contents can catch on fire.

Contents can burn skin.

Poison inside.

Design a Safety Poster

Design a poster that shows one thing to do to keep children safe around liquids and solids.

Can You Name It?

Write an example for each item below.

1. A solid that can melt. _____

2. A thick liquid. _____

3. A solid you see through. _____

4. A liquid you drink. _____

5. A solid you eat. _____

6. A liquid that can freeze. _____

7. A solid that is soft. _____

8. A sticky liquid. _____

9. A hard solid. _____

10. A clear liquid. _____

11. A solid that falls from the sky. _____

12. A liquid that falls from the sky. _____

13. A solid found in nature. _____

14. A liquid found in nature. _____

Make a Liquids and Solids Board Game

What You Need

- A base for the game board, such as a file folder or piece of cardboard
- Scissors
- Glue
- Note paper
- Coloring materials
- a pair of dice

What You Do

1. Choose a base for the game board.

2. Create a path the game pieces will follow. You may choose to give your path a shape: a U-shape, an L-shape, a square, or an oval. Make your path at least 50 squares long.

3. Outline a space to stack question cards cut from heavy paper. Print or handwrite questions on the cards.

4. Write instructions on some game board spaces.

5. Decorate the game board so people know what it is about.

6. Write the game rules.

7. Test the game with a friend. Is it too hard? Does it have enough spaces? Make your game better.

continued next page

Write the Rules

- How many people can play?
- How does a player move around the board?

  Here are some ideas:

  - roll the dice
  - answer a question on a card
  - follow the instructions on the game board spaces

Ideas for Game Cards

Create questions to test players' knowledge about

- liquids and solids
- floating and sinking
- safety

Create different categories such as

- true or false
- multiple choice
- explain something
- draw a picture

Ideas for Game Board Spaces

- Freeze! Lose a turn.
- Float 2 spaces ahead.
- Answer a question.

Simple Machines

Simple machines help you do work. They make work easier. Less push or pull is needed.

There are six simple machines.

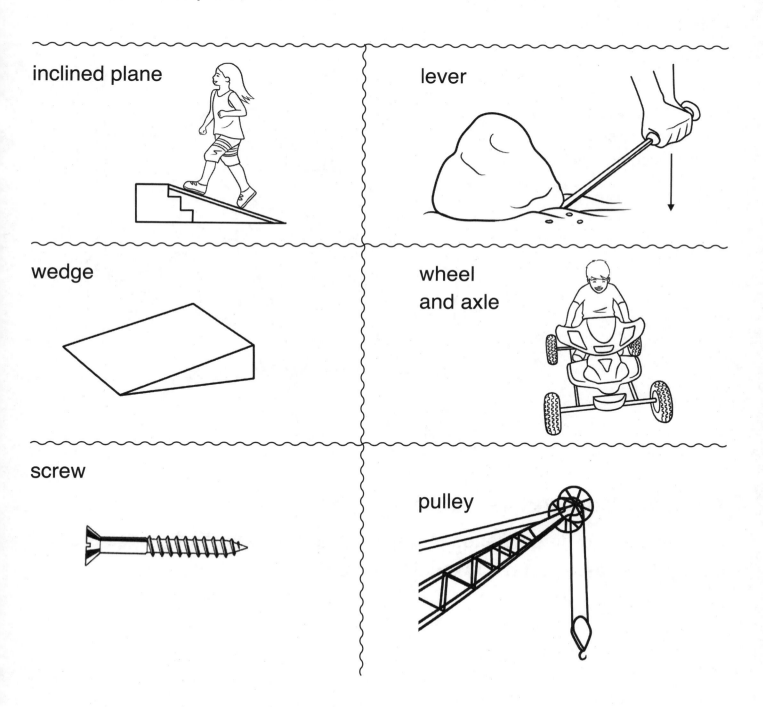

inclined plane

lever

wedge

wheel
and axle

screw

pulley

Inclined Planes

A ramp is an inclined plane. It connects a lower place to a higher place. Inclined planes make lifting easier. They are simple machines.

A heavy box can be moved up a ramp and into a truck. Ramps can also help move objects down.

It is difficult to lift a box straight up. Pushing the box up an inclined plane is easier.

There Are Many Inclined Planes

Cars drive on inclined planes to get to a bridge. Playground slides are inclined planes. A ramp for wheelchair users is an inclined plane.

"Inclined Planes"—Think About It!

1. A _____ is an inclined plane.

2. How does a ramp help furniture movers?

_____

3. Draw a picture of an inclined plane. Explain how it makes work easier.

_____

_____

_____

_____

Wedges at Work

Wedges are simple machines. They make work easier.
Wedges can do different things.

An axe is used to split wood.

The blade of a knife is a wedge.
It is used to cut food.

A doorstop is a wedge. You slip it under
a door to stop it from closing.

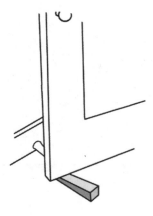

Did You Know?

Your front teeth are wedges. Wedges can cut up things. Your teeth cut
a bite of apple away from the rest of the apple.

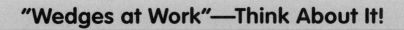

"Wedges at Work"—Think About It!

1. A wedge is made of one or two inclined planes ending in a

_____

2. An axe is a wedge. It is used for _____ .

3. A knife blade is a wedge. It is used for _____ .

4. A doorstop is a wedge. It makes the door _____ .

5. Think about wedges in your home. Give an example.

_____

6. How does a wedge make work easier?

_____

_____

_____

Screws

A screw is an inclined plane twisted around a rod. Screws can join, cut, lift, or push. Screws make work easier. They are simple machines.

Where Screws Are Used

Builders attach wood with screws.

Jars have lids that screw on. The screw shape holds the lid tight on the jar.

A jack lifts a car so you can change a tire. The jack uses a large screw.

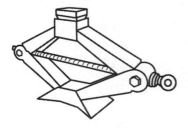

A twirling piano stool uses a screw. The seat twirls up and down.

Drill bits are shaped like screws to make holes in materials such as wood.

"Screws"—Think About It!

1. A screw is an _____ plane twisted around a

_____ .

2. Screws make work easier. List three examples.

_____

_____

_____

3. Think about screws at home. Give an example.

_____

4. How does a screw make work easier?

_____

_____

_____

Activity: Make a Look-Alike

1. Cut out the triangle below. Lay it on your desk. Put the long side at the bottom.
2. Put a pencil on top of the triangle, like this:

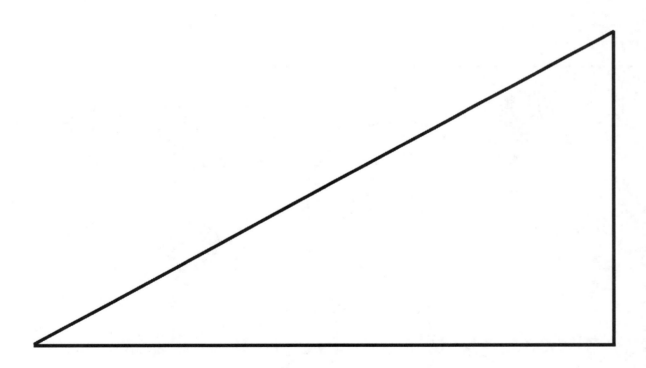

3. Wrap the paper around the pencil. Do this by slowly rolling the pencil.

4. What does this look like? _____

Levers

A lever is a simple machine. It moves a load. A load is the thing being moved. A lever is a bar. It balances on a support, or fulcrum. Moving the support changes how much effort is needed.

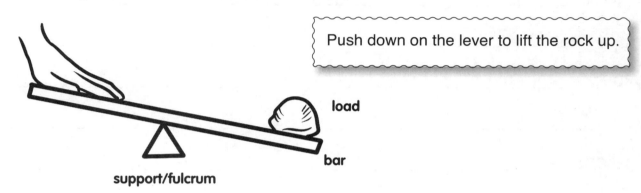

Push down on the lever to lift the rock up.

load

bar

support/fulcrum

Sometimes the support is in the middle of the lever. A seesaw in the park is a lever. The support on a seesaw is in the middle.

Sometimes the support is close to one end. A wheelbarrow is this type of lever. The wheel is the support. You pull up on the handles of a wheelbarrow. Moving a heavy load is easier in a wheelbarrow.

Did You Know?

Hockey sticks and baseball bats are levers. Your hands are the support for both of these levers.

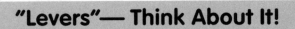

"Levers"— Think About It!

Define the following words.

1. lever _____

_____

2. load _____

_____

3. fulcrum _____

_____

4. What type of lever would you use to move a load of dirt?

_____

_____

_____

5. What lever can you find in the playground?

_____

_____

_____

6. Name a lever you use to a play sport.

_____

_____

_____

Wheels, Axles, and Pulleys

Wheels move people and things. A wheel can be attached to a rod called an axle. The wheel moves or spins on the axle. A wheel and axle is a simple machine.

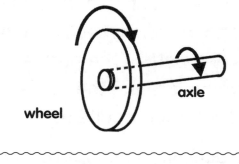

The wheel turns around the axle.

Wheels Around You

Wheels and axles help things move. Cars, trucks, and bicycles all have wheels and axles. The axles turn the wheels.

A doorknob is a wheel and axle. You turn the wheel (the doorknob). This turns the axle.

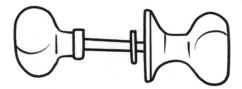

Gears

Some wheels have teeth around their edges. These wheels with teeth are called gears. As a gear turns, its teeth can make other gears turn. Gears can help move things. You can find gears in cars, bicycles, and washing machines.

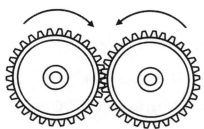

Pulleys

A pulley is a simple machine that can lift and lower or move a load. A pulley has two parts. One part is a wheel with a groove around the outside. The other part is a rope or chain.

It is difficult to carry a heavy box up a set of stairs. A pulley can help you move the box up. It can also help you lower a box.

You can raise and lower window blinds with a pulley.

Outdoor clothes lines have pulleys at both ends.

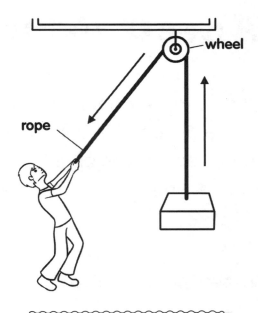

You pull down on the rope to lift the box.

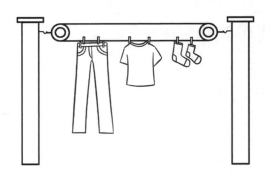

Activity: Wheels, Axles, and Pulleys Are Everywhere

1. Look through magazines and catalogs.
2. Cut out pictures of things that use wheels, axles, and pulleys.
3. Make a collage with the pictures and your own drawings. You can use words in the collage, too.

"Wheels, Axles, and Pulleys"—Think About It!

1. What is a pulley? _____

_____

_____

2. Circle the examples of a pulley.

    A. knives and hammers

    B. flag poles and clothes lines

    C. paper and pencils

3. Circle the two parts of a pulley.

    A. wheel and axle

    B. handle and bucket

    C. wheel and rope

4. How do pulleys help us?

_____

_____

_____

_____

___

Simple Machines Working Together

Some machines have simple machines in them.

Scissors

Scissors are made up of two levers and wedges. The two handles you squeeze are levers. The scissors cut because the blades are sharp-edged wedges.

Shovel

A shovel is also made up of a lever and a wedge. The blade is a wedge. It helps you cut into the ground. The handle is the lever. Your hands are the support, or fulcrum that the lever balances on. It lets you lift the dirt more easily.

Bicycle

A bicycle uses many simple machines. The wheels and axles on a bicycle are easy to see. Each brake is a set of levers. Gears make the wheels turn.

Living with Machines

Simple machines and devices make life easier for people. Machines help us get around. They help us move large and heavy things.

Machines Make Life Better

There are many ways machines help us. Wheelchairs allow people with disabilities to get around. Wheelchairs roll easily because they have wheels and axles. People in wheelchairs cannot roll up stairs. But they can roll up inclined planes.

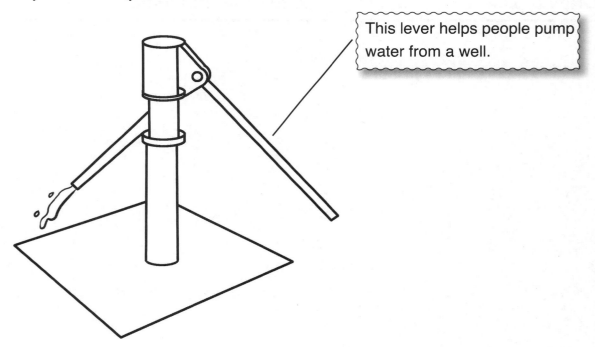

This lever helps people pump water from a well.

Simple machines and mechanisms make life more fun. Pianos use levers. When you press a key, a lever hits a string. This makes a sound. People also use machines such as treadmills to be fit and healthy. Treadmills have inclined planes that can make exercising more difficult or easier.

My Favorite Machine

1. Think about machines you use for fun. Which one is your favorite?

Tell why. _____

_____

_____

_____

2. Draw a picture of you using your favorite machine.

Get Moving!

When you run around your school yard, you are moving. When you spin around in a circle, you are moving. Jumping and swinging are other types of movement.

Objects move, too. A skateboard can roll. A ball can bounce.

When you move, you change where you are. You might move up or down, or backward or forward.

Sometimes you have to move an object. You have to change where it is. Maybe you have to move a box from outside to inside your bedroom. If the box is light, it is easy to move. But if the box is heavy, you need help.

Brain Stretch

Make a list of different ways that people can move.

Movement Word Search

You move in many ways. Machines also move in many ways.
Find these motions in the puzzle below.

F	O	R	W	A	R	D	X
R	J	U	M	P	S	J	R
O	P	W	L	S	W	O	U
L	U	A	E	P	I	G	N
L	S	L	A	I	N	P	S
U	H	K	P	N	G	U	K
P	D	O	W	N	X	L	I
B	O	U	N	C	E	L	P
B	A	C	K	W	A	R	D

backward   bounce   down   forward   jog   jump   leap   push
pull   roll   run   skip   spin   swing   up   walk

Match the Simple Machine

Match each simple machine to a description.

screw

lever

pulley

wheel and axle

wedge

inclined plane

made up of two parts—a circle and a rod

used to fasten or drill

can lift a heavy load by pushing on it

can be used for splitting things

looks like a ramp

pull down on a rope to make a load go up

Up and Down in Elevators

Elevators move people up and down in a building. An elevator is faster than using stairs. It makes work and life easier.

There were no elevators long ago. People did not build very tall buildings. It would take too long to climb stairs up a tall building. People would get tired.

Elevators were invented more than 150 years ago. Then people started to build very tall buildings. They put elevators in the buildings.

Outside an Elevator

There are two buttons outside an elevator door. They are called call buttons.

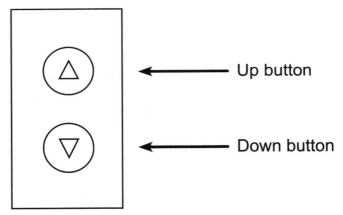

Up button

Down button

Press the top button if you want to go up. Press the bottom button if you want to go down. Soon the elevator doors will open.

Let people come out of the elevator before you go in.

continued next page

Inside an Elevator

There is a control panel inside the elevator. The control panel has buttons with numbers.

Press the number of the floor you want to go to. The door will close. Then the elevator will start to move.

The control panel also has elevator door buttons. Press the open button to keep the door open. Press the close button to make the door close right away.

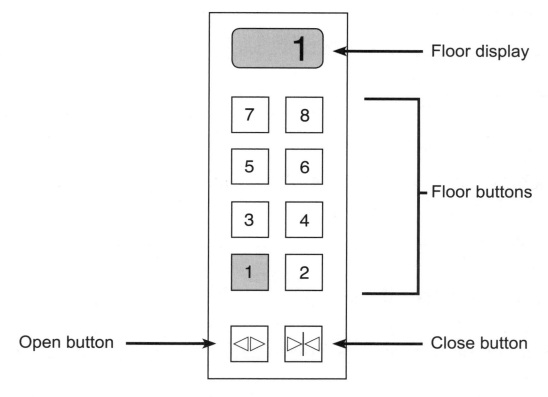

The elevator moves, then stops. The door opens. Is it time for you to get off the elevator? Look at the floor display to find out.

The floor display tells what floor the elevator is on. The number changes as the elevator moves up or down.

1. Why do tall buildings need elevators?

_____

_____

_____

2. Some people cannot walk. They use wheelchairs to move around. Why are elevators good for people who use wheelchairs?

_____

_____

_____

_____

3. Look at the elevator door buttons. What does each button do?

◁▷ This button keeps the door _____.

▷◁ This button makes the door _____.

4. Why might someone press the button to keep the elevator doors open?

_____

_____

_____

Helicopters

What Is a Helicopter?

A helicopter is a flying machine. It uses blades to fly. The blades spin round and round very fast.

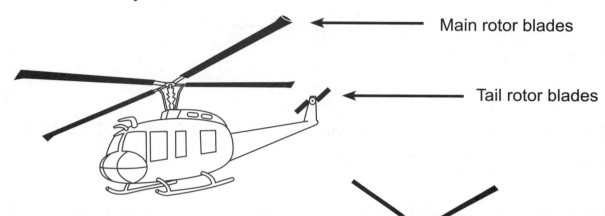

Main rotor blades

Tail rotor blades

What Jobs Do Helicopters Do?

Helicopters do many different jobs. Helicopters fly sick people to a hospital.

Helicopters move big, heavy objects.

Helicopters help put out forest fires. First they carry huge buckets of water to the fire. Then they dump the water on the fire.

continued next page 👉

How Are Helicopters and Airplanes Different?

An airplane has two large wings. Helicopters do not have wings.

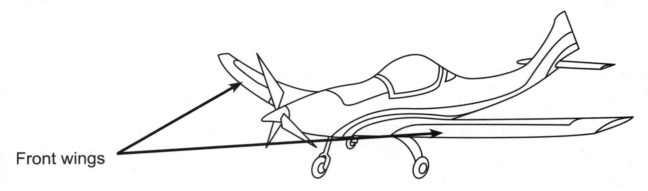

Front wings

Most airplanes do not have blades that spin round and round. Helicopters have blades on top and at the back.

Airplanes can fly very fast. Helicopters cannot fly as fast as airplanes.

Airplanes take off on a road called a runway. First they go faster and faster. Then they slowly lift up into the air.

Helicopters do not take off on a runway. They move straight up when they take off.

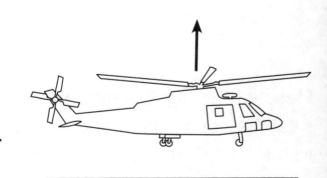

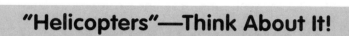

"Helicopters"—Think About It!

1. Fire trucks drive on roads. There might not be any roads in a forest. Why is a helicopter good for putting out forest fires?

_____

_____

_____

_____

2. Airplanes need wheels to start moving down a runway. Helicopters do not need wheels. Why not?

_____

_____

_____

_____

3. Would you rather fly in a helicopter or an airplane? Tell why.

_____

_____

_____

_____

Machines Need Energy

Machines need energy to work. Where does the energy come from?

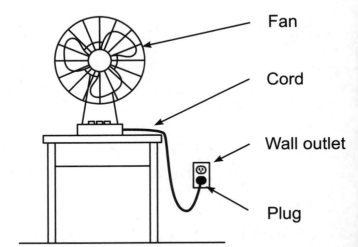

Fan

Cord

Wall outlet

Plug

Plug It In

Some machines have a plug at the end of a cord. The plug goes into a wall outlet. Energy from the wall outlet goes into the machine. Now the machine will work.

Be safe! Stay away from wall outlets. Ask an adult to put a plug into a wall outlet. Ask an adult to pull out a plug.

Use Batteries

Some machines do not have a cord with a plug. How do they get energy? They get energy from batteries.

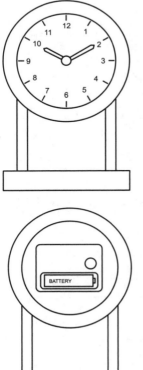

The energy in batteries gets used up over time. Then the machine stops working. It is time to put in new batteries.

Be safe! Ask an adult to put new batteries in a toy or machine.

continued next page ☞

Rechargeable Batteries

You can use rechargeable batteries over and over again. What happens when all the energy is used up? You can use a recharger. A recharger puts more energy into batteries.

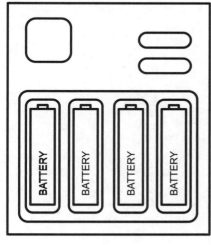

A recharger has a plug that goes into a wall outlet. Energy from the wall outlet goes into the batteries.

Front

Soon the batteries are full of energy again. They are ready to go back into a machine.

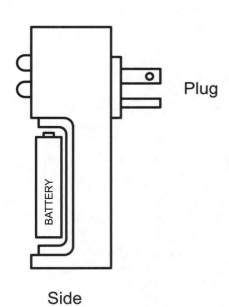

Plug

Be safe! Children should not use a recharger. Always ask an adult to recharge batteries.

Side

"Machines Need Energy"—Think About It!

1. Draw a machine that people use in your home. (Do not draw a machine that is shown in the article.)

2. Tell what the machine does.

____

____

____

3. How does the machine get energy to work? Put an **X** beside your answer.

_____ This machine gets energy from a wall outlet.

_____ This machine gets energy from batteries.

4. Write a list of 5 facts you have learned about how machines get the energy they need to work.

_____

_____

_____

_____

5. What happens to the energy in batteries over time?

_____

_____

6. What does a recharger do?

_____

_____

We Need Air!

All living things need air to stay alive. Air is made of gases. The gas we breathe in is oxygen. When we breathe out, we release a gas called carbon dioxide into the air. Most animals do this.

Did you know that the roots and leaves of a plant can take in air? Plants do the opposite of what you do! They take in carbon dioxide. This gas is in the air. Plants release oxygen back into the air.

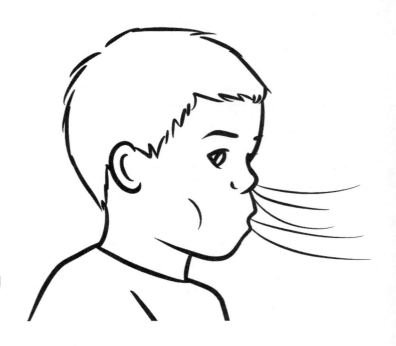

Think About It!

Fill in the blanks.

1. _____ is all around us.

2. No plants or animals can live without _____.

3. Air is made of _____.

4. The gas we take in is _____.

5. When we breathe out, we release _____.

6. Plants need to take in _____ from the air.

7. Plants release _____ back into the air.

Clean Air

It is important to have clean air to breathe.

Air that is not clean is polluted. Smog is air pollution. When there is smog, some people have trouble breathing. Pollution can make people sick.

Did you know that smog looks like smoke and fog?

NO IDLING

Children Breathing

Some people let their car engine run when they park. This is called idling. Idling releases gases that pollute the air. People can turn off their car engine to protect the air.

Gases from cars pollute the air. You can help keep air clean by driving less.

Think About It!

1. Think of two ways you can help keep air clean.

_____

_____

What Is Air?

We cannot see air, but it is all around us. The layer of air that surrounds Earth is called the atmosphere.

Air has no color. Air has no taste. Air has no odor. We might see dust in the air. We might smell a skunk in the air. But what we see and smell is not the air. We are seeing or smelling things that air carries.

Think About It!

Write five facts you learned about air.

1. _____

_____

2. _____

_____

3. _____

_____

4. _____

_____

5. _____

_____

Experiment: Does Air Take Up Space?

Try this experiment to find out whether air takes up space.

What You Need

- A clear plastic container
- Water
- A plastic cup (shorter than the container)
- A piece of paper towel

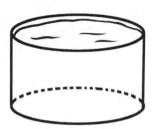

What You Do

1. Fill the container half full with water.
2. Crunch up the paper towel. Push it down to the bottom of the cup.
3. Turn the cup over. Make sure the paper towel does not fall out.
4. Predict what will happen when you push the cup into the water. Push the cup into the water. Do not tilt the cup.
5. Pull the cup straight out of the water. Then check the paper towel.

Think About It!

1. Was the paper towel wet or dry?_____
2. What kept the towel dry?

_____

_____

_____

Air Moves

Wind is air that is moving. Have you been outside on a windy day? Did you feel the air moving around you?

We can feel wind when air moves.

Read about how we use wind.

- Wind cools us down when we are warm.
- Wind makes flying a kite fun.
- Wind helps sailboats move.
- Wind spins a windmill to make electricity.
- Wind blows seeds. New plants grow where the seeds land.

Think About It!

1. What is moving air called? _____
2. List three ways we use wind.

_____

_____

_____

Air Moves at Home

We use moving air at home.

A hair dryer uses moving air to dry hair.

A dryer uses moving air to dry clothes.

A vacuum cleaner uses moving air to suck up dirt.

A fan keeps air moving. This makes you feel cooler.

Moving air can cool or heat your home.

• An air conditioner blows cool air to cool your home.
• A home furnace blows warm air. The moving air makes you feel warmer.

Think About It!

1. List three different ways you use moving air at home.

_____

_____

_____

Experiment: Make a Wind Sock

A wind sock tells which direction the wind is blowing from. Hang a wind sock where it catches the wind.

What You Need

- A medium-sized paper bag
- Glue
- Scissors
- Decorations (sparkles, stickers)
- Streamers (tissue paper or cellophane)
- A thick strip of construction paper
- Rope or strong string

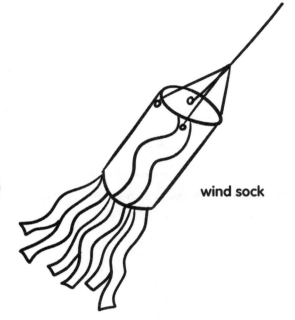

wind sock

What You Do

1. Cut off the bottom of the bag.
2. Decorate the bag.
3. Glue streamers around the bottom edge of the bag.
4. Glue the construction paper around the top edge of the bag.
5. Use the rope or string to hang your wind sock and test it.

Think About It!

1. How well did your wind sock work? Tell why you think so.

_____

_____

_____

Changes in the Air

The air moving around us affects the weather. Weather is the day-to-day conditions outside where you live.

A weather report tells about the weather outside. The report tells if it is warm or cold. It tells how windy or cloudy it is. It also tells if the air is dry or wet.

What do we do when the weather changes?

- When it is warm outside, we wear lighter clothes. We cool the air in our home using a fan or an air conditioner.
- When it is cold outside, we wear warmer clothes. We heat the air in our home with a furnace or fireplace.

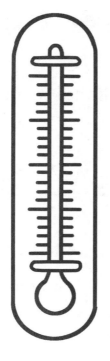

The temperature tells how warm or cold the air is. We can feel hot and cold air as the temperature changes.

Think About It!

1. On a sheet of paper, draw what you like to do outside. Show what you wear. Use a chart like this one.

Warm Weather	Cold Weather

How Does Wind Form?

The diagram shows how wind forms.

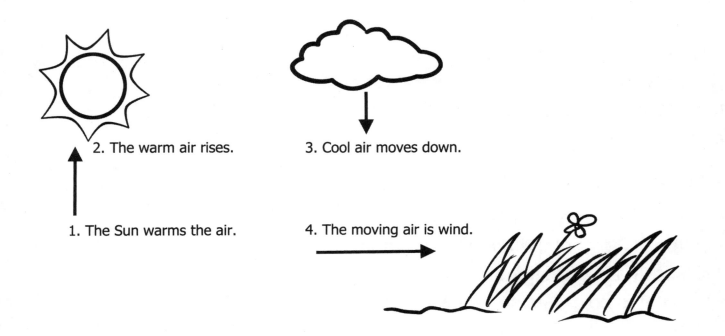

2. The warm air rises.

3. Cool air moves down.

1. The Sun warms the air.

4. The moving air is wind.

When wind moves fast, it can push you. Strong wind storms can blow down walls and break glass.

Did you know that a tornado is a storm with wind that moves in circles?

Look at the funnel shape of the tornado. A tornado is very dangerous. During a tornado, stay inside in a safe place such as a basement or hallway with no windows.

"How Does Wind Form?"—Think About It!

1. For each picture, tell how you know that air is moving.

Stay inside when there is a snowstorm.

_____

_____

Stay out of the water when the waves are too big.

_____

_____

Did you know that clothes dry quickly when it is warm outside?
Dry air and wind help dry clothes, too.

2. Which clothes will dry more quickly? Why do you think so?

A.

B.

_____

_____

_____

We Need Water!

All living things need water to live. People need to drink water every day to keep healthy. Water helps your body digest food. It keeps your body temperature steady. Water carries waste from your body. Most animals use water the same way we do.

Plants need water, too. The picture shows how plants get water.

Plants suck up water through their roots. They also take water in through their leaves, stems, branches, and trunks. Plants use the nutrients in water to make food.

Think About It!

Circle true or false.

1. Living things need water to live.   **True   False**

2. Animals do not need water.   **True   False**

3. Plants get water only through their roots.   **True   False**

4. List three ways that water helps your body.

_____

_____

_____

Water

Water comes in three forms or states of matter. These states are liquid, solid, and gas.

liquid

mountain stream

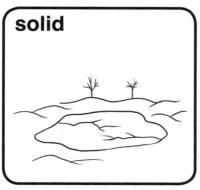

solid

frozen lake

gas

steam from hot springs

Water Is a Liquid: Most of the water we use is liquid. A liquid can be poured.

A liquid changes shape when it is poured into a container. Think about what shape it takes.

Think About It!

Circle true or false.

1. Water comes in two forms.   **True**   **False**

2. A liquid takes the shape of its container.   **True**   **False**

3. Rain and dew are liquids.   **True**   **False**

More About Water

Water Is a Solid: Sometimes we use water as a solid. Water becomes solid when it freezes. It is called ice.

Ice is hard. It cannot be poured. You can pick up and move a solid. Can you pick up a liquid?

Did you know that these are solids?

snow

frost

hail

Water Is a Gas: Water evaporates and changes into vapor when it is heated. Vapor is a gas. You cannot always see the gas in the air.

Did you know that fog and mist are not gases? They are actually tiny water drops in the air.

Water turns to a gas as it evaporates from clothes drying on a clothesline.

mist

fog

Write the state of matter for each example of water.

1. _____

hail

2. _____

fog

3. _____

water
evaporating
from drying
clothes

4. _____

rain

5. _____

ice

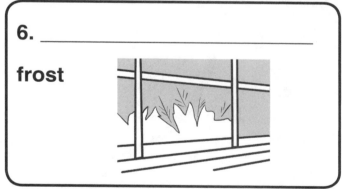

6. _____

frost

7. _____

snow

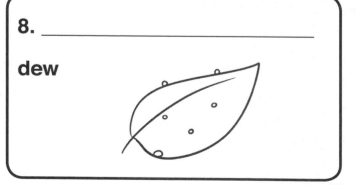

8. _____

dew

The Water Cycle

The water on Earth keeps recycling. We call this the water cycle. The water cycle makes sure that we always have water.

Read about the parts of the water cycle.

2. The air is cool high in the sky. The cool air makes the vapor change back to tiny drops of water. This is called condensation. The water drops group together. They form a cloud.

1. The Sun heats the water on Earth. Some of the heated water turns into vapor. This is called evaporation. The vapor rises into the air.

3. The water drops in the cloud become larger as more water condenses. When the cloud gets heavy, the water drops in the cloud fall back to Earth. The water falls as rain, hail, sleet, or snow. These are all forms of precipitation.

4. The cycle begins again.

"The Water Cycle"—Think About It!

1. Label the diagram of the water cycle. Use the words below.

condensation   evaporation   precipitation

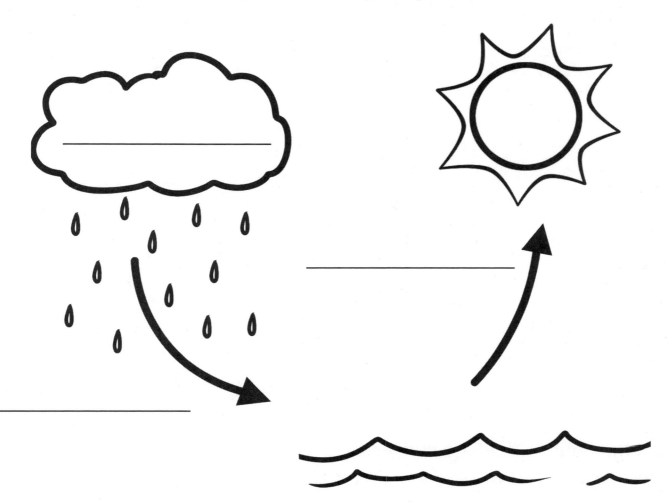

Fill in the blanks. Use the words below.

cloud   cool   heat

2. The _____ from the Sun changes water into vapor.

3. The _____ air changes vapor to tiny drops of water.

4. Water drops group together to make a _____.

Experiment: Make Your Own Water Cycle

Create the water cycle in your kitchen.

What You Need

- A pot
- Water
- A mirror
- A cup
- An oven mitt

SAFETY ALERT

Steam is hot. Wear the oven mitt to protect your hand.

What You Do

1. Ask an adult to help you boil water in a pot. When the water is hot, you will see steam. Steam is water vapor. This is evaporation.

2. Ask the adult to hold the shiny side of a mirror over the pot. You will see tiny drops of water form on the mirror. This is condensation.

3. Put a cup under the mirror. Collect the water drops as they fall from the mirror. This is precipitation.

"Experiment: Make Your Own Water Cycle"—Think About It!

Complete the sentences. Use the words below.

condensation   evaporation   precipitation

Then draw and label a diagram to show each part of the water cycle.

1. Water in a pot boils. Some water changes to steam. This is _____ .	
2. Tiny water drops form on the mirror. This is _____ .	
3. The water drops fall from the mirror. This is _____ .	

Brain Stretch

Do you know why the mirror in the bathroom fogs up after a shower? The vapor from the hot shower rises from the shower and covers the mirror. Since the mirror is colder, the vapor changes back to water. What is this part of the water cycle called?

Where Is the Water?

Water is all around us.

- Lakes, rivers, and streams are full of water.
- High in the sky, clouds contain tiny water drops.
- There is water under the ground, too. If you dig in a garden, you may find the soil is damp. There is water in the soil.

Where Do We Get Water?

well

water tower

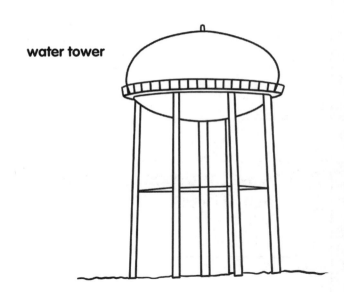

Some people get water from a well. Where do people who live in towns and cities get water?

Towns and cities hold water in reservoirs. A reservoir looks like a lake. Some reservoirs are created by people. A water tower is like a reservoir. Water leaves the reservoir through large pipes. It travels through many pipes before it gets to your home.

92

"Where Is the Water?"—Think About It!

Draw a picture to match each description.

1. Water in lakes and rivers	**2.** Water high in the sky
2. Water under the ground	**4.** Where we get water where I live

Did you know that water is treated? This makes water safe to use. You can help keep water clean. Here is one way.

Clean up after your pet. Pet waste can get into the water. This can make water unsafe.

How People Use Water at Home

Read how families use water at home.

drinking water	washing hands

flushing toilets	taking baths and showers
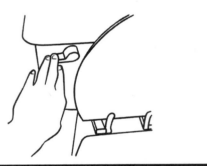	

washing and rinsing dishes	washing clothes
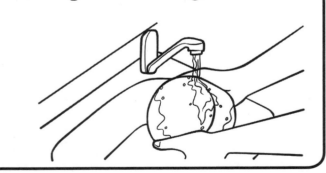	

Brain Stretch

We also use water for fun. Make a
list of ways you use water for fun.

scuba diving

94

"How People Use Water at Home"—Think About It!

1. Complete the web. Use what you have learned and your own ideas.

Ask an adult about how they use water at work.

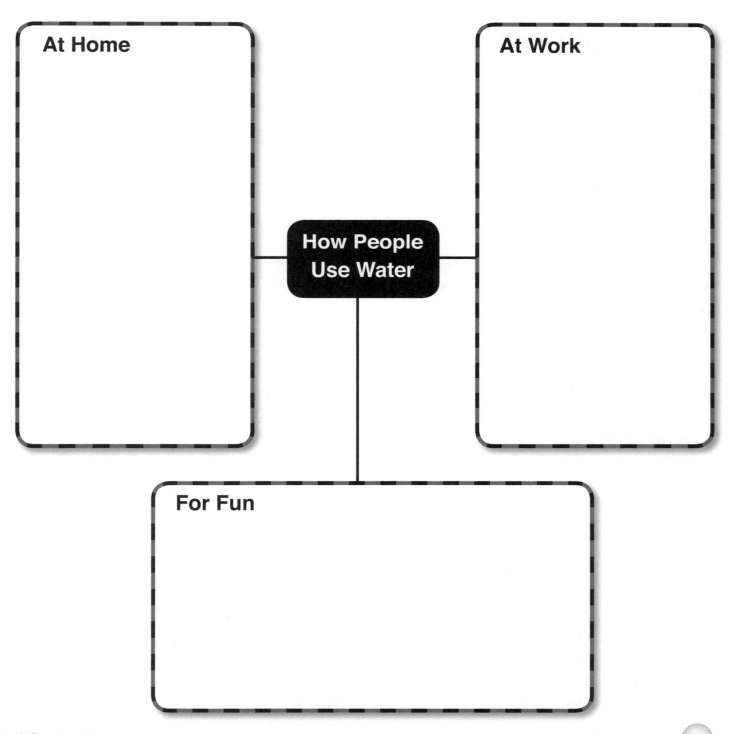

Use Water Wisely

We use a lot of water for drinking, cooking, and cleaning. How can we use water wisely?

Turn off the tap while you brush your teeth. Turn it on only for rinsing. Turn off the tap while your scrub your hands with soap, too.

Take a short shower instead of a bath. A shower uses less water.

Make sure you have a full load before using the dishwasher.

Do you want a glass of cold water? Do not let the tap run until the water is cold. Keep a bottle of water in the refrigerator. Then pour only as much water as you can drink.

Turn off the tap tightly after you use it. Small drips waste water.

Brain Stretch

Design a poster on tips for saving water.

Activity: How Much Water Do I Use?

Find out how much water you use.

What You Do

1. Choose one day. Each time you use water, put a checkmark in the chart.

How I Use Water	Number of Times in a Day
Drinking	
Washing hands	
Brushing teeth	
Flushing the toilet	
Taking a bath or shower	
Other	

2. Think about how you use water. What could you do to save water?

_____

_____

Weather Word Search

Circle the words about weather that you can find. Look for these words.

P	S	U	N	C	O	L	D	F	O	G
R	I	F	P	C	S	S	N	T	F	T
E	H	C	R	W	A	R	M	S	B	E
C	A	L	A	W	I	N	D	L	R	M
I	I	O	I	T	H	O	T	E	E	P
P	L	U	N	O	E	L	M	E	E	E
I	O	D	W	A	T	E	R	T	Z	R
T	T	O	R	N	A	D	O	F	E	A
A	D	E	W	A	O	M	I	S	T	T
T	L	I	C	E	S	N	O	W	A	U
I	T	I	M	E	B	L	O	S	I	R
O	B	O	I	C	I	T	A	E	R	E
N	S	T	O	R	M	F	R	O	S	T

air   breeze   cold   cloud   dew   fog   frost   hail
hot   ice   mist   precipitation   rain   sleet   snow   storm
sun   temperature   tornado   warm   water   wind

STEM-Related Occupations

To learn more about some of these occupations visit the following Websites:

www.sciencebuddies.org/science-engineering-careers

https://kids.usa.gov/watch-videos/index.shtml

Accountant
Aerospace Engineer
Agricultural Engineer
Agricultural Technician
Aircraft Mechanic and
    Service Technician
Animal Breeder
Animal Trainer
Animator
Anthropologist
Architect
Astronaut
Astronomer
Athletic Trainer
Audio Engineer
Audiologist
Automotive Mechanic
Biochemical Engineer
Biochemist/Biophysicist
Biologist
Biology Teacher
Biomedical Engineer
Business Owner
Cardiovascular Technician
Carpenter
Chef
Chemical Engineer
Chemical Technician
Chemistry Teacher
Chiropractor
Civil Engineer
Civil Engineering Technician
Climate Change Analyst
Clinical Psychologist
Computer Engineer
Computer Programmer
Computer Systems Analyst
Construction Manager
Counselling Psychologist
Dietetic Technician

Dietitian and Nutritionist
Doctor
Electrical Engineering Technician
Electrician
Electronics Engineer
Emergency Medical Technician
Environmental Engineer
Environmental Engineering Technician
Environmental Restoration Planner
Environmental Scientist
Epidemiologist
Fire-Prevention Engineer
Fish and Game Worker
Food Science Technician
Food Scientist and Technologist
Forest and Conservation Technician
Forest and Conservation Worker
Geoscientist
Graphic Designer
Hydrologist
Industrial Engineer
Interior Designer
Landscape Architect
Manufacturing Engineer
Marine Architect
Marine Biologist
Math Teacher
Mechanical Engineer
Mechanical Engineering Technician
Medical Lab Technician
Medical Scientist
Meteorologist
Microbiologist
Microsystems Engineer
Mining and Geological Engineer
Molecular and Cellular Biologist
Neurologist
Nuclear Engineer
Nursery and Greenhouse Manager
Nutritionist

Occupational Health and Safety Specialist
Optical Engineer
Optometrist
Paleontologist
Patent Lawyer
Pathologist
Park Ranger
Petroleum Engineer
Pharmacist
Physical Therapist
Physician
Physician Assistant
Physicist
Pilot
Psychologist
Registered Nurse
Respiratory Therapist
Robotics Engineer
Robotics Technician
School Psychologist
Seismologist
Software Developer (Applications)
Software Developer (Systems Software)
Soil and Plant Scientist
Soil and Water Conservationist
Space Scientist
Speech-Language Pathologist
Statistician
Transportation Engineer
Transportation Planner
Urban Planner
Veterinarian
Video Game Designer
Volcanologist
Water/Wastewater Engineer
Wind Energy Engineer
X-ray Technician
Zookeeper
Zoologist
Wildlife Biologist

STEM Jobs Word Search

Circle the STEM jobs in the puzzle. Use the word list below.

architect   astronaut   biologist   carpenter

chef   doctor   engineer   nurse   pilot

plumber   veterinarian   zookeeper

A	R	C	H	I	T	E	C	T	V
N	E	N	G	I	N	E	E	R	E
U	C	C	P	B	Z	A	Z	C	T
R	A	P	L	I	D	S	O	H	E
S	R	R	U	O	O	T	O	E	R
E	P	Q	M	L	C	R	K	F	I
P	E	N	B	O	T	O	E	P	N
V	N	P	E	G	O	N	E	I	A
I	T	G	R	I	R	A	P	L	R
T	E	M	Z	S	S	U	E	O	I
U	R	B	Z	T	O	T	R	T	A
X	D	Y	L	T	Q	W	B	R	N

What Is My Occupation?

Match the occupation to the correct description.

> **zookeeper   chef   pilot   dentist   carpenter**

1. I am someone who builds or repair things made from wood.

I am a _____

2. I am someone who cooks tasty food for people.

I am a _____

3. I am someone who helps take care of teeth and fixes them.

I am a _____

4. I am someone who takes care of wild animals and trains them.

I am a _____

5. I fly airplanes and take people to places far away.

I am a _____

continued next page ☞

Match the occupation to the correct description.

| plumber | animator | veterinarian | paleontologist | architect |

6. I am someone who designs and plans buildings.

I am a _____

7. I am someone who creates cartoons.

I am an _____

8. I am someone who studies prehistoric times.

I am a _____

9. I am someone who takes care of sick animals.

I am a _____

10. I am someone who can install and fix pipes that carry water, gas, or waste.

I am a _____

Be an Architect

An architect is someone who designs plans for a building such as a home, skyscraper, mall, school, or sports arena.

Design a building of your choice.

Describe your building.

What is the building?

_____

What is the building used for?

_____

_____

What makes the building special?

_____

_____

When I Grow Up...

Draw a picture of what you would like to be when you grow up.

I would like to be a _____.

Job Description

_____

_____

_____

_____

I want to be this when I grow up because _____

_____

_____.

Engineering in Our Daily Lives

Engineers design and build things that we use every day. Use magazines to cut out and paste pictures of things that make peoples lives easier. Some examples include a toothbrush or a video game.

Write about your collage.

_____

_____

Engineers Make Our Lives Better

Cut out and paste two pictures of things that make people's lives easier.

Complete the sentences.

I picked a picture of

_____.

I chose this because _____

_____

_____.

Complete the sentences.

I picked a picture of

_____.

I chose this because _____

_____

_____.

Think Like an Engineer!

An engineer is a person who designs and build things. Engineers want to understand how and why things work. Engineers try different ideas, learn from their mistakes, then try again. Engineers call these steps the design process.

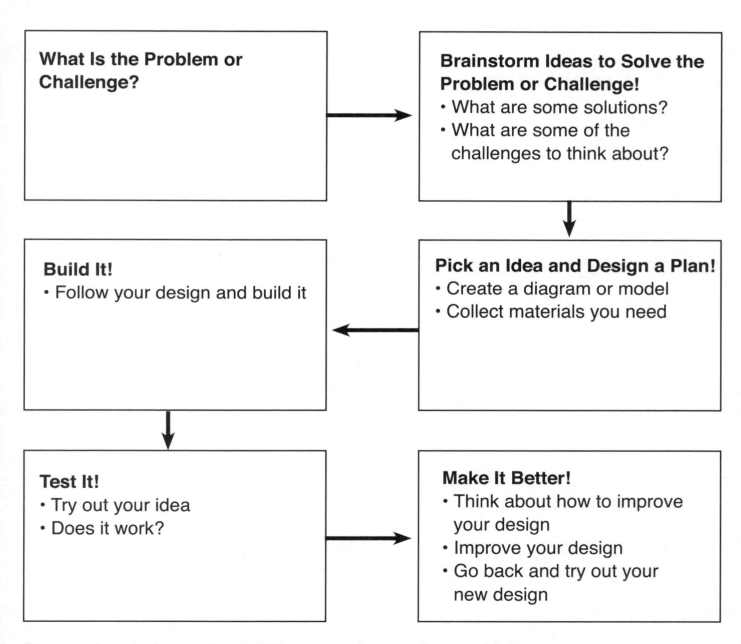

What Is the Problem or Challenge?

Brainstorm Ideas to Solve the Problem or Challenge!
- What are some solutions?
- What are some of the challenges to think about?

Build It!
- Follow your design and build it

Pick an Idea and Design a Plan!
- Create a diagram or model
- Collect materials you need

Test It!
- Try out your idea
- Does it work?

Make It Better!
- Think about how to improve your design
- Improve your design
- Go back and try out your new design

Remember to be patient. Take your time to figure things out.

The Design Process

1. What is the problem or challenge?

_____

_____

2. Think about it! What are some ideas to solve the problem or challenge?

_____

_____

_____

_____

_____

_____

continued next page ☞

3. Pick a design idea! Draw and label a picture of your design. Write about your plan.

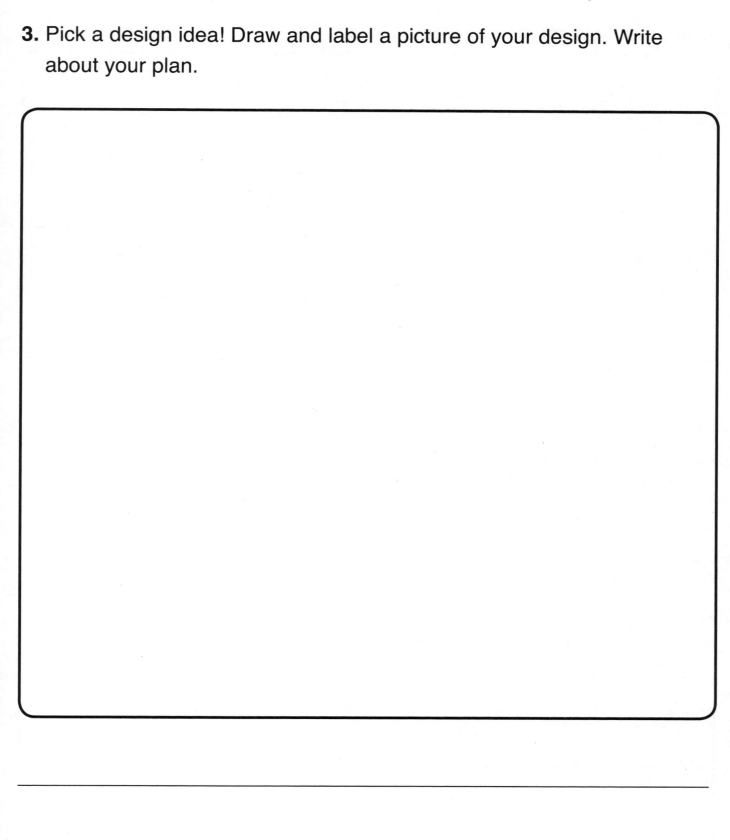

_____

_____

continued next page

4. Get ready! What materials do you need?

continued next page 👉

5. Test it! Build your design and try it out.

Did it work?   Yes ☐   A little ☐   No ☐

6. Make it better! How can you make your design better?

_____

_____

7. Try your design out again. What happened?

_____

_____

8. What do you wonder about?

_____

_____

9. What are you proud of?

_____

_____

STEM Vocabulary

Keep a list of new science words you have learned. Make sure to include the definition for each word.

Word	Definition

How Am I Doing?

	Completing my work	Using my time wisely	Following directions	Keeping organized
Full speed ahead!	• My work is always complete and done with care. • I added extra details to my work.	• I always get my work done on time.	• I always follow directions.	• My materials are always neatly organized. • I am always prepared and ready to learn.
Keep going!	• My work is complete and done with care. • I added extra details to my work.	• I usually get my work done on time.	• I usually follow directions without reminders.	• I usually can find my materials. • I am usually prepared and ready to learn.
Slow down!	• My work is complete. • I need to check my work.	• I sometimes get my work done on time.	• I sometimes need reminders to follow directions.	• I sometimes need time to find my materials. • I am sometimes prepared and ready to learn.
Stop!	• My work is not complete. • I need to check my work.	• I rarely get my work done on time.	• I need reminders to follow directions.	• I need to organize my materials. • I am rarely prepared and ready to learn.

STEM Rubric

	Level 1 Below Expectations	Level 2 Approaches Expectations	Level 3 Meets Expectations	Level 4 Exceeds Expectations
Knowledge of STEM Concepts	• Displays little understanding of concepts. • Rarely gives complete explanations. • Intensive teacher support is needed.	• Displays a satisfactory understanding of most concepts. • Sometimes gives appropriate, but incomplete explanations. • Teacher support is sometimes needed.	• Displays a considerable understanding of most concepts. • Usually gives complete or nearly complete explanations. • Infrequent teacher support is needed.	• Displays a thorough understanding of all or almost all concepts. • Consistently gives appropriate and complete explanations independently. • No teacher support is needed.
Application of STEM Concepts	• Relates science concepts to outside world with extensive teacher prompts. • Application of concepts rarely appropriate and accurate.	• Relates science concepts to outside world with some teacher prompts. • Application of concepts sometimes appropriate and accurate.	• Relates science concepts to outside world with few teacher prompts. • Application of concepts usually appropriate and accurate.	• Relates science concepts to outside world independently. • Application of concepts almost always appropriate and accurate.
Written Communication of Ideas	• Expresses ideas with limited critical thinking skills. • Few ideas are well organized and effective.	• Expresses ideas with some critical thinking skills. • Some ideas are well organized and effective.	• Expresses ideas with considerable critical thinking skills. • Most ideas are well organized and effective.	• Expresses ideas with in-depth critical thinking skills. • Ideas are well organized and effective.
Oral Communication of Ideas	• Rarely uses correct science terminology when discussing science concepts.	• Sometimes uses correct science terminology when discussing science concepts.	• Usually uses correct science terminology when discussing science concepts.	• Consistently uses correct science terminology when discussing science concepts.

Notes: _____

_____

_____

STEM Focus _____

Student's Name	Knowledge of STEM Concepts	Application of STEM Concepts	Written Communication of Ideas	Oral Communication Skills	Overall Grade

STEM Expert!

_____

Wonderful work!

Great Work!

_____

Keep up the effort!

Unit: Growth and Changes in Animals

Mammals Are Animals, pages 2–3
Sample answers:
1. born live, produces milk, warm blooded, has fur
2. cat, human, hamster
3. It has a long tail, whiskers, and likes being petted. (cat)

Other Kinds of Animals, page 4
As a class, discuss the different kinds of animals, their features, and where they live. Ask students for examples of other animals for each category.

Classify Animals Game, pages 5–6
Amphibians—frog
Birds—goose, duck, bluebird
Fish—goldfish, shark
Insects—ladybug, mosquito, bee, beetle, ant, butterfly
Mammals—Beluga whale, dog, deer, squirrel
Reptiles—lizard, snake, turtle, crocodile

Animals Grow Up, pages 7–9
1. From the top: tadpole, froglet, frog, eggs
2. four
3. C; 4. A; 5. D; 6. E; 7. B

Brain Stretch, page 9
Drawings should show the three stages of the chicken life cycle.

Animals Are Built to Live, pages 10–11
1. body adaptation
2. An adaptation is a different feature that helps an animal survive. Example: warm fur in a cold habitat
3. Answers will vary.

Body Coverings, pages 12–13
Sample answers:
1. shell and skin
2. The shell helps protect the turtle from predators.
3. cat
4. snake
5. bird
6. fish
7. frog
8. lobster
9. The quills prevent predators from biting or hitting the porcupine.

Animals Hide, pages 14–15
1. Animals use camouflage to blend in with their surroundings.
2. Color—polar bear, snowy owl, white-tailed deer
Both—bumblebee, giraffe, tiger
Patterns—zebra

Animals Adapt to the Seasons, pages 16–17
1. True
2. False
3. True
4. Migrate (red)—butterfly, deer
Hibernate (blue)—squirrel, bear
Coat changes colour (green)—Arctic fox, Arctic hare

Animals Help Us, pages 18–19
1. Sample answer:
   • provide food
   • provide companionship
   • provide materials to make things
   • compost plant material
   • protect plants
   • help plants reproduce
   • guide people
   • carry things
2. Cows give people meat to eat and milk to drink. Their hide gives leather to make things.
3. Bats and dragonflies eating mosquitoes reduces the mosquito population, which means fewer bites and less spread of disease.

Animals Can Harm Us, pages 20–21
1. D, 2. G, 3. E, 4. A, 5. C, 6. B, 7. F

Helpful or Harmful? page 22
1. happy
2. sad
3. happy

Animals in Danger! pages 23–24
Sample answers:
1. sea otter
2. Looks—cat-sized furry swimmer
Lives—ocean coastline
Eats—clams and sea urchins
Features—long body and tail, short legs, and long whiskers
Interesting fact—eats while floating on its back
Why endangered—hunting (historical)
To help protect it—clean up habitat
3. Answers will vary.

Unit: Properties of Liquids and Solids

Matter Is Everywhere, page 25
1. liquid, solid, gas
2. Sample answer: table
3. Sample answer: milk
4. Sample answer: air

Solids, page 26
1. Sample answer: brick
2. Sample answer: foam
3. Sample answer: tree
4. Yes, a baseball is a solid because the facts about solids are true for a baseball.

Solids Collage, page 27
Create a bulletin board display of students' collages.

Liquids, page 28
1. Sample answer: vinegar
2. Sample answer: nail polish
3. Sample answer: dew
4. Yes, paint is a liquid because the facts about liquids are true for paint.

Liquids Collage, page 29
Create a bulletin board display of students' collages.

Experiment: Will It Change? page 30
Ask student volunteers to share their findings with the class.

Compare and Contrast, page 31
Ask student volunteers to share their findings with the class.

Experiment: Mix It Up, page 32
Dissolved—sugar, salt, and baking soda

Experiment: Big Stuff, page 33
Expanding ice pushed the foil cap off the bottle.

Experiment: Sink or Float? page 34
Sink: marble and coin
Float: feather and paper
The button may float depending on the material and shape.

Experiment: Soak It Up! page 35
Absorb—sponge, cloth, paper
Repel—waxed paper, plastic
Most to least absorbent: sponge, cloth, paper, waxed paper, plastic

Experiment: The Layered Look, page 36
Expected results: Corn syrup forms the bottom layer, water in the middle, and cooking oil floats on top. The cork floats on the surface (oil), the toy, building block, and raisin float between the corn syrup and water, and the ice cube floats between the water and oil.

Rain and Sleet, page 37
Create a bulletin board display of students' stories, or ask for volunteers to share with the class.

Liquids and Solids Every Day, page 38
Sample answers:
1. bread, salt, granola bar, soap
2. water, juice, mouth wash

Stay Safe, pages 39–40
1. Safety symbols warn people about the dangers of a substance so that they know to protect themselves when using it, and that it needs to be stored and disposed of safely.
2. A different container would not have the safety symbols and would not say what was in the container.
3. Hand—Contents can burn skin.
Fire—Contents can catch on fire.
Skull and crossbones—Contains poison.

Design a Safety Poster, page 41
Create a bulletin board display of students' safety posters.

Can You Name It? page 42
Sample answers:
1. butter
2. maple syrup
3. window glass
4. milk
5. bread
6. juice
7. ice cream
8. honey
9. candy
10. water
11. snow
12. rain
13. ice
14. sap

Make a Liquids and Solids Board Game, pages 43–44
When students are finished creating their board games, assign pairs or small groups to play the games.

Unit: Simple Machines

Simple Machines, page 45
Discuss the examples of simple machines as a class. Ask students for examples of when they have ever used each simple machine.

Inclined Planes, pages 46–47
1. ramp
2. A ramp helps furniture movers push or pull heavy objects on the ramp instead of lifting them.
3. Answers will vary.

Wedges at Work, pages 48–49
1. sharp edge
2. splitting wood
3. cutting
4. stay open
5. Sample answer: doorstop
6. The inclined planes make a sharp edge that is used to cut things apart or separate two things.

Screws, pages 50–51
1. inclined, rod
2. Sample answer: augers cut holes, screws join materials together, screws reduce the effort needed to push the rod through the material
3. Sample answer: toothpaste cap
4. Turning the object, which pushes the rod, is easier than pushing the rod itself.

Activity: Make a Look-Alike, page 52
4. Students should say that it looks like a screw.

Levers, pages 53–54
1. A bar that balances on a support and moves a load.
2. The object that is moved.
3. The point on which the rod balances.
4. Sample answer: shovel or wheelbarrow

5. Sample answer: see-saw
6. Sample answer: hockey stick

Wheels, Axles, and Pulleys, pages 55–57
1. A simple machine made of a grooved wheel and a rope.
2. B. flagpoles and clotheslines
3. C. wheel and rope
4. Pulleys make it easier to lift or lower a load.

My Favorite Machine, page 60
You might wish to make a bulletin board display of students' machines.

Brain Stretch, page 61
Accept all reasonable responses.

Movement Word Search, page 62

F	O	R	W	A	R	D	X
R	J	U	M	P	S	J	R
O	P	W	L	S	W	O	U
L	U	A	E	P	I	G	N
L	S	L	A	I	N	P	S
U	H	K	P	N	G	U	K
P	D	O	W	N	X	L	I
B	O	U	N	C	E	L	P
B	A	C	K	W	A	R	D

Match the Simple Machine, page 63
screw—used to fasten or drill
lever—can lift a heavy load by pushing on it
pulley—pull down on a rope to make a load go up
wheel and axle—made up of two parts—a circle and a rod
wedge—can be used for splitting things
inclined plane—looks like a ramp

Up and Down in Elevators, pages 64–66
1. It would take too long to climb lots of stairs. People would get tired.
2. People who use wheelchairs cannot use stairs.
3. *Top button:* This button keeps the door open. *Bottom button:* This button makes the door close.
4. *Sample answers:* Someone might press the button to keep the doors open if someone is coming to get in the elevator or if someone wants to get off the elevator and the door is starting to close.

Helicopters, pages 67–69
1. A helicopter is good for putting out forest fires because it does not need to drive on roads. It can fly to a fire.

2. Helicopters do not need wheels because they fly straight up when they take off.
3. Invite students to share and compare their responses.

Machines Need Energy, pages 70–73
1. Some students might draw machines with a plug (e.g., desktop computer, microwave, lamp), while others might draw machines that use batteries (e.g., flashlight, computer mouse, toy).
2. You could invite students to share their responses. Confirm with them that the machine needs a source of energy to function.
3. Where necessary, explain to students that some machines contain rechargeable batteries that are not visible (e.g., laptop computer, electric toothbrush, hand-held vacuum devices) and the battery is recharged when the machine is plugged into a wall outlet.
4. Students should list any five of the following facts: Some machines have a plug at the end of a cord. The plug goes into a wall outlet. Then energy goes from the wall outlet into the machine to make it work. Some machines without a cord and plug use batteries to get energy to work. The energy in batteries gets used up over time. The batteries can be replaced. Some batteries can be put into a recharger that plugs into a wall outlet. Energy from the wall outlet goes into the batteries. When the batteries are full of energy, they are ready to go back into the machine to make it work again.
5. The energy in batteries gets used up over time.
6. A recharger puts more energy into batteries.

Unit: Air and Water in the Environment

We Need Air! page 74
1. air
2. air
3. gases
4. oxygen
5. carbon dioxide
6. carbon dioxide
7. oxygen

Clean Air, page 75
1. Sample answer: You can help keep air clean by driving less (walk, take the bus, or bike) and planting trees and other plants that clean the air.

What Is Air? page 76
Sample answers:
1. Air is all around us.
2. We cannot see air.
3. We cannot smell air.
4. We cannot taste air.
5. Atmosphere is the layer of air that surrounds Earth.

Experiment: Does Air Take Up Space? page 77
1. dry
2. The air in the cup kept the water out.

Air Moves, page 78
1. wind
2. Sample answer: To fly kites, to make electricity, and to make sailboats move.

Air Moves at Home, page 79
1. Sample answer: clothes dryer, hair dryer, fan on stove sucks smoke away

Experiment: Make a Wind Sock, page 80
1. Ask students how their wind sock worked. If it did not work, ask how they could improve it.

Changes in the Air, page 81
1. Sample answer:
Warm Weather wear—shorts, T-shirt, hat, sandals
Cold Weather wear—wool hat, snowsuit, sweater, gloves, scarf, warm socks, snow boots

How Does Wind Form? pages 82–83
1. I can see snow blowing around. Moving air is pushing the water into big waves.
2. B. The clothes in picture B will dry more quickly because warm wind is blowing across the clothes.

We Need Water! page 84
1. True
2. False
3. False
4. Digestion, temperature control, and waste removal.

Water, page 85
1. False
2. True
3. True

More About Water, pages 86–87
1. solid   5. solid
2. liquid   6. solid
3. gas   7. solid
4. liquid   8. liquid

The Water Cycle, pages 88–89
1. top—condensation; middle—evaporation; bottom—precipitation
2. heat
3. cool
4. cloud

Experiment: Make Your Own Water Cycle, pages 90–91
1. evaporation
2. condensation
3. precipitation

Brain Stretch, page 91
condensation

How People Use Water at Home, pages 94–95
1. Discuss students' answers as a class.

Brain Stretch, page 94
Ask student volunteers to share their ideas of ways to use water for fun.

Brain Stretch, page 96
Create a bulletin board display of students' tip posters.

Activity: How Much Water Do I Use? page 97
2. Have students share their ideas for how to save water.

Weather Word Search, page 98

STEM Jobs Word Search, page 100

What Is My Occupation? pages 101–102
1. carpenter   6. architect
2. chef   7. animator
3. dentist   8. paleontologist
4. zookeeper   9. veterinarian
5. pilot   10. plumber